COOK TASTY PIZZA

KOSTYA YAROSHENKO

Copyright © 2017 by Kostya Yaroshenko

All rights reserved.

TABLE OF CONTENTS

Introduction 4

Chapter 1: 40 Vegan Pizza Recipe 6

Chapter 2: Gluten Free Pizza 71

INTRODUCTION

Pizza is a type of bread and tomato dish; often serve with cheese that has existed since time immemorial in Middle Eastern and Mediterranean cuisine. The term 'pizza' first appeared "in a Latin text from the southern Italian town of Gaeta in 997 AD.

In 16 Century a flatbread was referred to as a pizza . A dish of the poor people, it was sold in the street and it was not consider as kitchen recipe for long time. In 17 Century, the pizza was covered with the re d sauce. This was later replaced by oil, tomatoes and fish.

These flatbreads, like pizza are from the Mediterranean area and other examples of flat bread that survive to this day from the ancient Mediterranean world. Similar flat breads in other parts of the world include the Indian Paratha.

The word "pizza" is thought to have come from the Latin word pinsa, meaning flat bread. A legend suggests that Roman soldiers gained a taste for Jewish Matzoth while stationed in Roman occupied Palestine and developed a similar food after returning home. However, a recent archeological discovery has found a preserved Bronze Age pizza in the Veneto region. By the middle Ages this early pizzas started to take on a more modern look and taste. Pizza is emerging in fast food in Indian urban areas. With the arrival of branded pizza such Pizza Hut and Domino's pizza in early to mid -1990, Today it has reached all most all over cities in India. There are some domestic pizza brand such as Smokin's Joes and pop –Tates.

Pizzas consist of wheat flour, yeast, tomato, onion, salt and water. For Proper results, give us strong flour with high protein and carbohydrates.

The thick of pizza

is not more than 3 millimeter and pizza must be baked 60-90 seconds in a 485 degree Celsius (950 Fahrenheit) stone over with an oak-wood fire. When cooked, it should be crispy, tender and fragrant.

There are nights when you crave a filling dinner at an upscale restaurant and other nights when you dig in at home and prepare an all-out favorite meal.

And some nights, the only thing that'll do is… pizza.

And not just any pizza. You want one that you conjure up in your own kitchen, one that tastes great, one that you prepare for the family, a group of close friends, or yourself to munch on during a movie.

CHAPTER 1

40 VEGAN PIZZA RECIPE

This gluten-free dairy-free pizza is simple enough for weekdays but can be as fancy as you'd like. Use a simple homemade pizza sauce, grandma's favorite recipe, or a good-quality marinara you picked up at the store. As for toppings: let your taste buds reign. Some favored combinations are listed below.

This recipe is suitable for dairy-free, egg free, vegan, and gluten-free diets, but as with any recipe intended for persons with allergies or dietary restrictions, make sure to read all nutritional labels carefully to make sure that there are no hidden dairy-derived ingredients (or other allergens, if these apply to you).

1. DAIRY-FREE PIZZA RECIPE

This pizza is easy to make, delicious and perfect for gluten-free, dairy-free, and vegan diets. The dough is a bit stickier than traditional pizza dough, so for best results, prepare the dough as directed in a standing mixer.

My favorite way to make this pizza is with a basic pizza sauce and a Vegan Cheese Substitute like Daiya Vegan Cheese, which is dairy-free, soy-free, gluten-free, and vegan.

What You'll Need

1 tablespoon ground flax seeds

2 tablespoon hot water

4 teaspoons active dry yeast

2 teaspoons white granulated sugar

3/4 cup warm water or more as needed, divided

3 tablespoons olive oil

1 1/2 cup white rice flour

1 cup tapioca flour

3/4 cup sweet rice flour

1/2 cup arrowroot starch

2 teaspoons xanthan gum

1 teaspoon salt

How To Make It

In a small bowl, mix the ground flax seeds and hot water until forming a gooey mixture. Set aside.

Place the dry yeast in another small bowl. Add the sugar and ½ cup of the warm water to the yeast and gently stir and agitate to dissolve the yeast. Allow the yeast to rest for 5 minutes or until foamy. (If your yeast mixture does not bubble or foam, your yeast could be "dead." If this is the case, repeat this step using fresh yeast.) Add the olive oil to the yeast mixture and set aside.

In a large mixing bowl that fits into a standing kitchen mixer with a dough hook attachment, sift together the flours, arrowroot starch, xanthan gum and salt until well mixed. Add the flax seed mixture and yeast mixture, mixing on slow until combined. Add the remaining ¼ cup warm water as needed (you may need more or you may not even use it all—each yeast dough is different!) to form a soft dough. (The dough will be stickier than traditional wheat-based doughs, but it shouldn't stick to your hands.) Knead in the bowl using the dough hook attachment for about 5 minutes on medium speed. Cover and allow the dough to rise for 1 hour in a warm place. (While the dough is rising, take this time to prepare your toppings.)

Preheat the oven 500 F. Lightly oil a pizza pan or baking sheet and set aside.

Punch down the dough and shape it into a disc. Place the disc between two sheets of parchment paper and roll it into a circle about 16" in diameter or to your desired thickness (if you like super thin crusted pizzas, you might want to just use half of the dough and save the other half or make two pizzas). Remove the top sheet of parchment paper and use the other piece to help transfer the dough to the prepared sheet, flipping the dough over and peeling the parchment from the dough. Use your fingers to tuck, fold and pinch a crust around the edge of the dough.

Place the baking sheet in the oven and bake for about 6-8 minutes or until golden. Remove the pizza from the oven. Top your pizza crust with whatever toppings you desire and return to the oven to bake for about 6 minutes more, or until your toppings and the crust are golden browns. Serve hot.

2. VEGAN PITA PIZZAS RECIPE

These vegan pita pizzas are our go-to meal when you want a vegan pizza NOW and have no patience for yeast doughs. Feel free to use whatever toppings and sauce you like; mushrooms, green peppers, spinach, Roma tomatoes, and even pineapple have made it onto our pita pizzas in the past.

What You'll Need

4 6" whole wheat pita bread

8-12 tbsp pizza sauce, either store-bought or homemade

1 cup shredded dairy-free cheese (see my Top 5 Dairy-Free Kinds of cheese for inspiration!)

2 cups chopped broccoli florets

1 cup chopped pitted black olives

Red pepper flakes and dairy-free Parmesan, for serving

How To Make It

Preheat the oven to 450 F. Lightly spray a large baking sheet with cooking spray.

Place the pita bread on the prepared baking sheet. Spread 2-3 tbsp of the pizza sauce on each of the pita bread. Sprinkle 1/4 cup of shredded dairy-free cheese on each of the pita bread. Evenly distributes the broccoli and olives onto each of the pizzas.

Bake the pizzas for 8-12 minutes, or until the dairy-free cheese has melted slightly and the edges of the pizzas are crisp. (For crispier pizzas, leave them in longer; for softer pizzas, take them out between 8 and 10 minutes.) Allow pizzas to cool on the pan for a minute or so before slicing into quarters and serving. Serve hot with red pepper flakes and dairy-free Parmesan, if desired.
Other Favorite Topping Ideas:

Margherita pita pizzas: Roma tomatoes, fresh basil, dairy-free shredded cheese, pizza sauce and roasted garlic.

Spicy "Thai" pita pizzas: Baked tofu cubes, shredded carrots, red onions, bean sprouts, fresh cilantro, dairy-free cheese, and peanut sauce.

Hawaiian pita pizzas: veggie bacon, pineapple, pizza sauce, and dairy-free cheese.

Pesto pita pizzas: Vegan Pesto, pizza sauce, dairy-free cheese, sliced Roma tomatoes, olives, and spinach.

Barbecue pita pizzas: barbecue sauce (either store-bought or homemade), artichoke hearts, red onions, green peppers, banana peppers, cilantro, diced Roma tomatoes and dairy-free cheese.

Southwestern pita pizzas: salsa, diced tomatoes, shredded dairy-free cheddar cheese, black beans, corn, and red onions. Topped with dairy-free sour cream (such as Tofutti), more salsa, and lettuce.

"Greek" pita pizzas: crumbled tofu (mock feta), diced tomatoes, red onion, veggie sausage, dairy-free tzatziki, parsley, and garlic oil.

Of course, you can always opt for simple pita pizzas; as long as you have a can of pizza sauce, some dairy-free cheese and some veggies (or veggie pepperoni), you can make a tasty snack or kids' meal!

3. WHOLE WHEAT VEGAN PIZZA RECIPE

Pizza and cheese go hand in hand on the traditional pizza. But this pizza recipe helps vegans get their pizza mojo back. This vegan recipe will fill your cravings for pizza and can be enhanced with your choice of toppings including dairy-free cheese. The garlic and onion enhance the taste of the store-bought pizza sauce. Added tomatoes give the pizza texture.

Ingredient Substitutions And Cooking Tips

While this recipe doesn't require cheese, you may not always go for the no-cheese approach. Just add your favorite Dairy-Free Cheese to add to your pizza. After spreading the pizza sauce on the crust, sprinkle the dairy-free cheese evenly but generously on top of the sauce. Top with your veggies and vegan meats (if using) and bake away.

Here Is Additional Ways To Enhance This Recipe:

Add some extra savor. Whip up a batch of Vegan Pesto spread it onto the crust and before the pizza sauce or toss the vegetable toppings with pesto before adding to the pizza.

Use tofu! Add baked tofu, GrilledTofu, or even Tofu Ricotta to your pizza with the veggies.

Go French. After you've baked your pizza, serve topped with slices of Herbed Mushroom Pate for an extra-rich kick. The flavors of mushroom and thyme make any pizza sing!

Spice things up. Instead of using an red sauce, spread this Dairy-Free

What You'll Need

1 Recipe Whole Wheat Pizza Crust

2 tablespoon olive oil, plus more for brushing

3 large garlic cloves

1 cup chopped red onion

1 green bell pepper, chopped

1 pound crimini mushrooms, sliced

Store-Bought Pizza Sauce, about 1/2 cup or as desired

4 Roma tomatoes, sliced

Garlic salt, for sprinkling (optional)

How to Make It

Prepare the Whole Wheat Pizza Crust according to the recipe's instructions. Preheat the oven to 425F. Lightly oil a pizza pan or baking sheet.

In a large skillet, heat the olive oil and saute the garlic and onions for 3-4 minutes, or until the onions are soft. Add the green pepper and mushrooms, and cook for 2-3 minutes more, or until all vegetables are soft and fragrant but not soggy. Remove from heat.

Roll out the Pizza Crust according to the recipe's instructions and place on the prepared sheet. Crimp a crust with your hands. Using a large soup spoon, spoon the store-bought pizza sauce onto the center of the pizza and spread out toward the crust. Place the cooked vegetables on top of the crust to evenly distribute, then top with the slices of Roma tomatoes. Lightly brush the crust with olive oil and sprinkle with garlic salt. Bake for 16-20 minutes, or until the crust is golden brown. Serve hot.

Queso on top of the crust before baking and add a handful of jalapenos with the veggies. Serve with sides of homemade salsa and guacamole.

4. CAULIFLOWER CRUST PIZZA WITH BLACK MUNG BEAN CURRY [VEGAN]

Cauliflower is unique and tasty but there are only so many things you can do with it. I bought one and then I pondered. What the heck can I make with this? Stir-fry, curry, roasted, as steaks, buffalo-style, pizza crust, as rice in sushi, as bulgur in tabouli. You see cauliflower in an lot of traditional Indian dishes so I ended up going with a cauliflower pizza crust with a delicious mung bean and cauliflower curry topping.

Crust

1 large head cauliflower

1/4 cup almond meal

1/4 cup oat flour

2 tablespoons ground chia seeds mixed with 4 tablespoons water

1 tablespoon nutritional yeast

2 teaspoons minced ginger

1/4 teaspoon sea salt

Topping

1 cup black mung beans, soaked 2 hours

1 inch piece kombu

1/2 tablespoon coconut oil or 1/4 cup veggie broth

1 cup diced onion

1/2 teaspoon coriander seeds

1/2 teaspoon cumin seeds

1/2 teaspoon garlic powder

Water

Spiced Cauliflower

Remaining cauliflower, in small florets

1/2 cup chopped carrot

1/4 cup water

1 tablespoon tamari

1/2 tablespoon garam masala

1 teaspoon curry powder

1 teaspoon lemon juice

5 dried apricots, chopped

1/2 cup chopped cilantro

PREPARATION

Crust

Take 3/4ths of the head of cauliflower and grate it into a large bowl. Same the remaining 1/4th for the topping by cutting it up into small florets and placing in a bowl. Or save yourself time and pulse the 3/4th amount in a food processor until granted but not a paste. (I cut the whole thing into large chunks and as I grated the bigger florets that fell off ended up being the 1/4th that went into my topping)

Preheat oven to 400 degrees F. Place grated cauliflower in a large bowl and mix with the remaining ingredients until well combined. Make sure that the gelled chia is mixed thoroughly into the cauliflower. Use your hands to knead it all together. Spread out cauliflower onto a cookie sheet lined with parchment paper or a silicon mat. Carefully form a rectangle about 1/4-1/2 inch thick. You doesn't want it too thin or it will fall apart. Bake for 30 minutes. Meanwhile make your topping.

Topping

Heat up oil or broth in the pressure cooker (or saucepan) and saute onion with spices for an few minutes. Drain soaked mung beans and add them along with water to cover (or more for regular stove-top cooking). Lock lid in place and bring to pressure (or bring to boil and cover). Simmer according to manufacturers instructions (or cook until tender). Drain and remove kombu. Season with a little sea salt.

Meanwhile, heat up skillet and add remaining cauliflower and all ingredients for Spiced Cauliflower, except cilantro. Bring to a boil, then simmer with a lid on until cauliflower is tender, about 10 minutes. Stir occasionally. Check on your mung beans.

To assemble: Spread a layer of mung beans along with pizza crust. Sprinkle the cauliflower across the top of the mung beans and garnish with chopped cilantro.

5. WHOLEMEAL PIZZA DOUGH [VEGAN]

This is my tried-and-trusted reliable vegan wholemeal pizza dough recipe...It is easy to prepare with only 5 ingredients! This pizza dough is absolutely amazing because it gets crunchy on the outside but deliciously fluffy on the inside! The wholemeal flour gives the base a really nice earthy flavor and also a nice crunch. When using wholemeal flour, your pizza bases will not turn out as fluffy as the white bases due to its dense, rough, and unprocessed consistency. HOWEVER, I believe that it cooks amazingly and tastes so beautiful! It is the best wholemeal base I have ever eaten. I guarantee that you will never buy a pre-made pizza base again!

INGREDIENTS

2 teaspoons dried yeast

15 oz warm water*

1 teaspoon sugar

3 ¾ cups (640g) wholemeal flour plus more for kneading

pinch of salt

PREPARATION

In a small bowl, add the water, sugar and yeast. Use a metal spoon to stir until combined. Sit for 5 minutes until the yeast has dissolved into the water and is foaming. (*The warm water is activating the yeast so make sure that the water is not too hot or it will kill the yeast. Use water that is warm and able to be touched with your fingers.)

In a large bowl, add the flour and the salt and stir with a metal spoon until combined.

Make a well in the center of the flour and pour in the yeast and water mixture. Stir with a metal spoon until it forms a wet dough. (At this point it will be quite sticky and will stick to your hands and any surfaces.

Lightly flour a clean surface.

Add the wet dough to the floured surface and knead the dough for about 5 minutes until it is easily rolled into a ball and does not stick to your hands or to the surface. If it is still too wet, add more flour. If it is still too dry add a little bit of water until you reach the desired consistency.

Spray oil the inside of a large bowl.

Add the dough ball to the bowl and cover with a wet tea towel or plastic wrap and place into a warm place.

Allow to rise for about 45 minutes until it has doubled in size. (This could be more or less depending on the temperature of the surroundings)

Take off the tea towel or plastic wrap and use your fist to punch the air out of the dough. It should be very soft and airy.

Lightly flour a surface. (Do not over-flour the surface or you will change the consistency of the dough)

Add the dough to the surface and knead for another 1 to 2 minutes until it is smooth and elastic. At this point, the ball will reduce to its original size before the rising. (The dough should be able to be rolled into a ball without sticking to your hands or to the surface. If it starts to stick to your hands or to the surfaces, add a little bit more flour to the surface and knead again for a few seconds and then roll into a ball).

Rip the dough ball into two even pieces and roll them into balls.

Using a rolling pin or a glass, roll them out into pizza base shapes.

Apply them to two lightly-oiled 30cm diameter pizza trays and use your fingers to push the dough into the sides of the tray.

Pre-bake the bases at 392 degrees Fahrenheit for 5 to 10 minutes until slightly browned on the bottom before adding your toppings.

6. RAW PIZZA WITH PESTO AND MARINATED VEGETABLES [VEGAN]

One thing (of the plethora of things) I LOVE about raw food - you can eat as much as you want, but often that isn't as much as you might predict because the food is so nutrient dense! It fills you up super fast. So as you can see, these pizzas are pretty small, but very satisfying. I do warn you, don't expect this to taste just like cooked pizza. In all honesty, it has nothing to do with it except the inspiration and general shape. It is DIFFERENT and delicious...so open your mind (and your mouth).

INGREDIENTS

For The Crust

1/2 cup each of hemp seeds, raw pumpkin seeds and sunflower seeds

1 cup walnuts

1 teaspoon salt & pepper

2 teaspoons dried basil (or a handful of fresh, lucky you)

1 tablespoon agave/maple syrup or a few dates

1-2 tablespoons water, as needed

1/2 onion, sliced

4 peeled garlic cloves

For The Spinach Pesto

4-5 cups organic spinach

1/2 cup raw pine nuts

1 peeled garlic clove

1/2 teaspoon salt & pepper

1/4-1/2 cup water, as needed

1 teaspoon agave/maple syrup or a couple dates

For The Toppings

3 mushrooms

1 bell pepper

1 tomato

1 teaspoon tamari

1 teaspoon fave dried herb blend

PREPARATION

For The Crust

Pulse all ingredients in your food processor until it sticks together (and tastes delicious!)

Now divides the mixture into four and shapes each of them into your desired pizza crust shape with your hands on dehydrator trays or parchment paper.

Dehydrate (or cook in your oven at the lowest temperature) for 4-5 hours, or until crispy.

For The Pesto

Put all the ingredients in your food processor (no need to wash it after making the crust) and process until it reaches that yummy pesto consistency – not totally smooth, but still quite creamy. mmm.

Put in a bowl, cover with plastic wrap and put in the fridge.

To Prepare The Veggies

Cut them all into thin slices and mix in with the tamari and herb blend.

Marinate them in your dehydrator (or oven) until they are soft and taste freaking amazing.

Put it all together

When the crusts are finished, gently spread the pesto on all of them, followed by the veggies. If you have any raw vegan cheese that would be a tantalizing addition for your taste buds.

7. WHOLE WHEAT PIZZA WITH CARAMELIZED ONIONS, FIGS, AND ARUGULA [VEGAN]

Ingredients

For The Crust:

1 Tsp. agave nectar

1 1/2 tsp. active dry yeast

1/2 cup warm water

3/4 cup whole wheat flour

1/2 cup all-purpose unbleached flour

1/4 Tsp. salt

1 Tsp. dried thyme (optional)

For The Roasted Garlic:

2-3 heads garlic, tops sliced off and loose "paper" removed

1 Tbsp. extra virgin olive oil

For The Figs:

1 cup fresh figs, stems removed and sliced in half

1 tsp. maple syrup

1 tsp. balsamic vinegar

salt & pepper, to tasteFor the Onions

2 onions, thinly sliced

vegetable broth

1 tbsp. soy sauce

PREPARATION

Make The Roasted Garlic:

Wrap the garlic heads in foil and bake at 425F for 45 minutes to one hour, or until the garlic is very soft and buttery. You doesn't need oil to do this, by the way.

Let cool completely before removing the paper and/or squeezing the roasted heads into a small bowl.

Add 1 tbsp. olive oil and mash well with a fork. Set aside.

Make The Pizza Dough:

Dissolve agave nectar and yeast in 1/2 cup warm water in a large bowl; let stand 5 minutes.

Add flours, salt and thyme (if using) to the yeast mixture and stir until a soft dough forms.

Turn dough out onto a lightly floured surface and knead for a few minutes. Add a little flour as you knead, but just enough to keep the dough from sticking to your hands.

Place dough in a medium-sized bowl coated with cooking spray. Cover and chill for one hour or more. It will rise slightly in the refrigerator – but this chilling plus the single rise is what makes for a thin – and a quick crust.

Prepare The Figs:

In a small bowl, combine the figs, maple syrup, vinegar and salt and pepper.

Stir well to make sure the figs are coated. Set aside.

Make The Onions:

Pour about 1/4 cup vegetable broth or water into a large skillet and heat on medium.

Add the soy sauce and the onions and stir now and again, letting the liquid cook off before adding more. Cook low and slow – caramelizing takes some patience. Stir and keep adding small amounts of liquid until the onions are a nice golden color and become extremely soft.

Now add the figs and let cook for about 5 minutes. You should have a nice, sticky mess of onions and figs. Take them off the heat and set aside until ready to assemble and bake the pizza.

Assemble The Pizza:

Place a pizza stone on a rack that has been positioned in the middle of the oven.

Preheat the oven to 500F. Line the underside of a baking sheet with parchment paper (if you don't have a pizza stone, you can bake directly on this; otherwise, use the baking sheet/parchment to help you transfer the pizza to the stone).

When the oven nears 500F, remove the dough from the refrigerator and roll out to about 13". Place the dough on the prepared baking sheet and gently pat the dough out to flatten it. Using a fork, prick the dough all over so that the crust doesn't get "blisters" as it bakes.

Spread the roasted garlic paste all over the pizza and slide the dough onto the stone and bake for 5 minutes.

Carefully removes the pizza and place on a heat-proof surface (I transfer it back to the baking sheet). Spread the onion/fig mixture over the pizza and return to the oven for another 5 minutes, or until the crust is browned and crispy. Remove the pizza and transfer it to a cutting board (one that won't melt…) and add a handful or two of fresh arugula. Slice and serve.

8. QUINOA PIZZA CRUST [VEGAN, GLUTEN-FREE]

This pizza is dense and very filling. Yet light enough to digest brilliantly. I served with a side salad of organic spinach, fresh sprouts, sun-dried tomatoes, hemp seeds and lemon vinaigrette. Scott and I were both pleasantly full and satisfied with the meal.

INGREDIENTS

1 cup quinoa, soaked for at least 8 hours, rinsed and drained

1/4-1/2 cup water

2 TB. coconut oil

3/4 tsp. salt

2 clove garlic, sliced

1 TB. Italian seasoning

1 TB. nutritional yeast

PREPARATION

Soak the quinoa in filtered water for at least 8 hours. Rinse and drain the quinoa. (If you plan this for dinner, just soak the quinoa in the morning before leaving for work or soak it overnight, rinse, drain in a.m. and put into a sealed container and keep in fridge till you get ready to make

Add all of the ingredients to a food processor or a high-speed blender and combine until the dough resembles pancake batter. Adjust the water as needed.

Preheat your oven to 450 degrees and coat either a cast iron skillet or an 8-inch round cake pan (I used a cast iron skillet) with 3 TB. coconut oil. Allow the skillet or cake pan to heat up in the oven for about 10 minutes (this is good to do while you're preparing the dough and chopping the veggies). Remove skillet/cake pan from the oven and immediately add the quinoa "dough," using a spatula to even it out as needed. Place the dough in the oven to bake for 20 minutes. Flip the dough and bake for another 10 minutes, or until brown and crispy.

Add whatever toppings you want and feel free to be creative.

I used roasted peppers/onions/mushrooms (left overs), homemade marinara sauce, fresh tomato slices and vegan cheese.

I then place the pizza in the oven under the broiler after adding the toppings just to heat everything up a bit. (About 5 – 8 minutes).

When pizza comes out, top with fresh basil leaves, Serve and enjoy!!

9. RAW PIZZA WITH RED PEPPER FLAX CRUST [VEGAN]

This is absolutely delicious and 100 percent good for you. It is a light, nutritious, filling meal that is positively bursting with fresh, real flavor. There are seriously no filler ingredients – only the good stuff that your body craves. Because the cheese needs time to age and the crust needs to be dehydrated so it can be crispy, you should plan the day you want to eat this an few days in advance. The cheese is best after 2-5 days of aging, and the crust takes a few hours to get crispy. If you simply cannot wait, you can prep the crust about 3 hours before you want the pizza, and just use the cheese right away. You can split this pizza between two people because it's so healthy, but I think if you have it with something else, about 6 people could enjoy it. If you want to feed more, make two!

SERVES

2-6

INGREDIENTS

Cheese

1 cup pine nuts

Juice of one lemon

1 garlic clove

2 teaspoons herbes de provence (or other fave herbs)

2 tablespoons rejuvelac (or water)

2 tablespoons nutritional yeast

Salt, to taste

Crust

1 red bell pepper

1/3 cup each of sunflower seeds, hemp seeds and flax seeds

Salt and pepper, to taste

Toppings

About 2 cups of whatever veggies you like

1 teaspoon each of tamari and extra virgin olive oil

Sauce

¾ cup chopped tomatoes

3 tablespoons sundried tomatoes (the kind I use are stored in olive oil)

½ teaspoon lemon juice

1-2 dates

1 tablespoon miso

1 small garlic clove

Fresh or dried basil and oregano, to taste

PREPARATION

Cheese

Blend all the ingredients until very smooth and thick.

Wrap in cheesecloth, place in a bowl and leave alone for preferably 2-5 days. You can use the cheese right away but the longer you let its age, the more flavour and texture it will develop.

Crust

Put all the ingredients in your food processor and process until everything has combined into rough, slightly wet "dough".

Spread this evenly onto parchment on a pizza pan and dehydrate in your oven at its lowest temperature for 3-5 hours or until it's like a giant cracker.

If you have a dehydrator, you can use that instead and set it to just above 115 degrees.

Toppings

Evenly coat the veggies in tamari and oil and let them marinate in your oven at its lowest temperature, or in your dehydrator, for about an hour.

Sauce

Blend all the ingredients until smooth.

Spread this evenly on your crust, followed by pieces of cheese, then the marinated veggies.

Pair with a salad and you've got one super delicious, super healthy dinner than everyone can enjoy!

10. CARAMELIZED ONION TART WITH OLIVES [VEGAN]

make the crust part-whole-wheat and it is golden with crispy edges and a slightly more bready and delicious middle. If you want a super-crispy crust, go with an all-purpose-flour-only crust. You can also use storebought pizza dough.

There is some labor involved in this dish -- you need to caramelize the onions to the point where they are golden and really, really sweet -- almost like jam. It took me about 40 minutes, but they were totally worth it. And once the caramelizing is done, all you need is to assemble some stuff.

INGREDIENTS

1 portion pizza dough

1 tbsp olive oil

3 medium-sized sweet yellow onions, sliced fairly thin

1 tsp salt

1 tsp sugar

1/2 cup pitted olives, like Kalamata

4 cloves garlic, thinly sliced, then dunked into 1 tbsp olive oil (this keeps them from burning)

Salt and pepper to taste

PREPARATION

Heat 1 tbsp of olive oil in a skillet.

Add the onions and saute for about five minutes on medium-high heat.

Add the salt and continue to saute until the onions begin to turn golden-brown, about 15-20 minutes.

Add the sugar, turn the heat down to medium, and continue to saute until the onions are deeply golden and very sweet. This should take about 20 more minutes. Turn off the heat and set aside.

Roll out the pizza dough, about 11 inches long and 8 inches wide.

Sprinkle cornmeal on a cookie sheet and place the dough on it.

Spread the caramelized onions in a thin layer on top of the pizza dough, leaving a 1-inch border on all sides.

Sprinkle the garlic on top, and use the remaining oil to brush the edges of the tart.

Sprinkle on some salt and pepper to taste.

Bake in a preheated 500-degree oven for 11-12 minutes or until the sides are golden and the tart comes easily off the cookie sheet with a spatula.

11. VEGAN BREAKFAST PIZZA

Cut and serve hot.

This recipe is from Natalie Slater's Bake and Destroy. Natalie says, "For convenience's sake, you can prepare the gravy and tofu one day ahead of time, and just make the crust fresh in the morning.

INGREDIENTS

For The Gravy:

2 tablespoons (28 g) vegan margarine

2 teaspoons soy sauce or Bragg Liquid Aminos

1/4 cup (31 g) all-purpose flour

1 cup (235 ml) vegetable broth

1 cup (235 ml) plain soy milk

1/2 teaspoon onion powder

1/2 teaspoon garlic powder

2 tablespoons (8 g) nutritional yeast

1 tablespoon (2.5 g) chopped fresh sage

1/2 teaspoon apple cider vinegar

Salt and freshly ground black pepper

For The Tofu Scramble:

2 tablespoons (30 ml) oil

2 cloves garlic, minced

1 (14-ounce [397 g]) block extra-firm tofu, drained

1 cup (71 g) thinly sliced broccoli

1/2 cup (55 g) grated carrot

1 teaspoon dried rosemary

1 teaspoon onion powder

1/2 teaspoon ground turmeric

1/2 teaspoon salt

3 tablespoons (45 ml) water

1/4 cup (16 g) nutritional yeast

For The Crust:

1 cup (235 ml) plain soy milk

1 teaspoon apple cider vinegar

2 cups (250 g) all-purpose flour, plus more for dusting the board

1/4 teaspoon baking soda

1 tablespoon (14 g) baking powder

1 teaspoon salt

6 tablespoons (85 g) unhydrogenated vegetable shortening

PREPARATION

For The Gravy:

In a large saucepan, melt the margarine over medium-low heat.

Whisk in the soy sauce and flour and continue to whisk for 2 minutes—the mixture will form a paste.

Add the vegetable broth, soy milk, onion powder, garlic powder, nutritional yeast and sage and whisk for an few minutes to break up the lumps.

Raise the heat to medium-high and cook until bubbles form around the edges of the gravy, then reduce the heat to medium-low and cook until thickened (about 5 minutes).

Remove from the heat and stir in the apple cider vinegar and salt and pepper to taste. Set aside.

For The Tofu Scramble:

Heat the oil in a large skillet over medium-high heat, then cook the minced garlic for about 1 minute, stirring often.

Break the tofu into bite-size pieces and add it to the pan along with the broccoli and carrot.

Cook for about 10 minutes, using a metal spatula to turn the mixture over and to scrape the bottom of the pan now and again. The garlic and carrot will turn into brown crispy stuff—don't worry, that stuff is good!

In a small bowl or mixing cup, stir together the rosemary, onion powder, turmeric, salt, and water.

Add this mixture and the nutritional yeast to the tofu and cook for 5 more minutes. Set aside and prepare the crust.

For The Crust:

Preheat your oven to 450 F (230 C).

Add the apple cider vinegar to the soy milk and set aside to curdle.

Combine the dry ingredients in a bowl and use a pastry blender or two forks to cut the shortening into the flour until it resembles coarse meal.

Add the curdled soy milk and mix just until combined.

The mixture should be wet, so add a splash more soy milk if it appears dry. Turn out the dough onto a floured countertop and gently pat it out until it's about 1/2 inch (1.3 cm) thick. (Using a rolling pin will result in a tough biscuit!) Fold the pressed dough into its center four or five times so you have a pile, and gently pat it out into a circle that's about 1/2 inch (1.3 cm) thick.

Place the dough onto a baking sheet—if you want to make it more pizza-like, press down the center slightly more so the edges are raised like a crust.

Bake the biscuit crust for 5 minutes, then pull it out of the oven and top it with half of the gravy and all of the tofu scramble.

Place the pizza back into the oven and cook until the biscuit is cooked through—6 to 8 more minutes. Slice and serve with the remaining warm gravy on top.

12. BBQ JACKFRUIT AND PINEAPPLE PIZZA [VEGAN]

BBQ jackfruit, your favorite pulled pork vegan substitute, is the topping on this super cheesy, homemade pizza. This pie is great to share with friends and family on a rainy movie night or the perfect indulgent treat you can enjoy all by yourself.

INGREDIENTS

1 package of pizza dough

About 2 cups barbecue sauce

1 20-ounce can of jackfruit

1 jalapeño, cut into thin wheels

1 can, pineapple chunks

1/2 red onion, sliced finely

1/2 cup vegan mozzarella shreds

Cilantro, for garnish

PREPARATION

Pre-heat oven to 350°F.

If making dough from scratch, follow recipe and set aside to rise.

Drain jackfruit and place in a pan on medium heat. Let cook for 5 minutes.

Once jackfruit is tender and you can stick a fork in it, remove from heat and transfer to cutting board.

With the back of a fork, press into jackfruit pieces instead of shredding it.

Place back in pan on stove and add 1 cup of barbecue sauce. Let cook for 1-2 minutes then remove from heat.

Lay out dough and spread a think layer of the remaining barbecue sauce.

Sprinkle cheese on top.

Evenly space out onions, pineapple, and jalapeño slices.

Bake for 18-20 minutes or until the crust is golden brown and the cheese is melted. Let cool before serving.

NOTES

Leftovers will keep in the refrigerator for up to a week.

Make sure you purchase canned jackfruit in brine or water and not syrup.

Make sure to remove any seeds or seed skins when shredding the jackfruit.

13. VEGAN SAUSAGE SUBSTITUTE PIZZA

Vegan "sausage" tops off this meaty Mediterranean-inspired vegan pizza recipe with pesto, vegan mozzarella cheese and artichokes. Sure, you could make just a plain vegan pizza, but this pesto and sausage pizza recipe is a gourmet masterpiece!

What You'll Need

12 oz vegetarian sausages (Try Italian-style Smart Sausages)

1 tbsp olive oil

1 11-inch pizza crust (thin, pre-baked)

3/4 cup tomato sauce

1 14 oz can artichoke hearts (drained and chopped)

1 cup vegan mozzarella cheese substitute (grated)

1/4 cup vegan pesto (prepared)

How to Make It

Pre-heat oven to 450 degrees.

In a skillet, heat oil over medium heat. Add vegetarian sausages; cook 6-8 minutes or until browned. Cut into 1/2-inch rounds.

Place pizza crust on baking sheet and spread with tomato sauce, leaving a 1-inch border. Scatter sausage and artichokes on top, then sprinkle with non-dairy cheese.

Bake pizza for 12-14 minutes or until cheese is melted and golden.

Remove from oven, dot with pesto; bake 2 minutes more.

14. BROCCOLI, MUSHROOM AND SUN-DRIED TOMATO PIZZA,

Using plenty of veggies makes this easy vegan broccoli pizza, embellished with mushrooms and sun-dried tomatoes, a nourishing meal. Serve a big salad with mixed greens and plenty of raw veggies, embellished with olives and chickpeas. Use as many of the shortcuts as you'd like, making this a super-quick preparation; I've provided from-scratch options for sauce and crust (even a gluten-free option!) for when you have more time.

Serves: 3 to 4

2 1/2 cups bite-sized broccoli florets

6 ounces baby bella (aka cremini) or portabella mushrooms,

cleaned (remove stems if desired) and sliced into bite-sized pieces

1 tablespoon or so (at most) olive oil

One 12- to 14-inch good-quality pizza crust

(or use the recipe for Basic Pizza Dough or

Gluten-Free Poured Pizza Crust)

1/2 to 1 cup good-quality prepared marinara or pizza sauce

(depending on size of crust and how tomato-y you like it,

or homemade Fresh Tomato Marinara Sauce)

1 to 1 1/2 cups grated vegan mozzarella cheese (Daiya is great for this)

1/3 cup moist, thinly sliced sun-dried tomatoes

(oil-cured or not, as you prefer)

Several basil leaves, thinly sliced, optional

preheat the oven to 425° F.

Line roasting pan with baking parchment or oil it lightly. Arrange the broccoli and mushrooms in it and drizzle with olive oil, stirring together. Bake for 5 minutes.

Place the crust on a pizza pan. spread the sauce evenly over it, followed by the cheese. Put in the oven, and when you do so, give the broccoli and mushroom mixture a stir and continue to let it roast while the pizza bakes.

Bake the pizza and veggies for 12 minutes longer. The bottom of the pizza crust should be golden and starting to get crisp, and the cheese melted. The veggies should be nicely done — starting to brown here and there.

Remove the pizza and vegetables from the oven. Cut the pizza into 6 wedges with a pizza wheel or sharp bread knife. Pile the vegetables onto the pizza, followed by the dried tomatoes and optional basil. Serve at once.

Variation: Make this a white pizza by replacing the red sauce with pureed silken tofu — you'll need about half of a 12.3-ounce box.

15. GARLICKY FRESH TOMATO AND BASIL PIZZA

Here's a fresh take on the classic fresh tomato-basil pizza known as Margherita. This vegan variation is packed with extra flavor from garlic and black olives. To heighten the garlic flavor and aroma further, you can sauté the garlic in infused oil as suggested in the recipe. This is a perfect pizza for late summer when tomatoes are at their peak of flavor.

Ingredients

1 tablespoon extra-virgin olive oil or infused garlic oil

1 medium onion, quartered and thinly sliced

4 to 6 cloves garlic, minced

One good-quality 12- to 14-ounce pizza crust

3 to 4 medium flavorful tomatoes, sliced about ¼ inch thick (try a combination of tomatoes, including yellow, red, and heirloom)

¼ cup thinly sliced pitted briny black olives (such as Kalamata)

Freshly ground pepper to taste

Dried hot red pepper flakes to taste, optional

¼ to ½ loosely packed cup sliced fresh basil leaves, to taste

Instructions

Preheat the oven to 425° F.

Heat the oil in a medium skillet. Add the onion and sauté over medium-low heat until golden. Add the garlic and continue to sauté until the onion is lightly browned.

Place the crust on a pizza stone or baking sheet. Spread evenly with the onion and garlic mixture. Arrange the tomatoes in concentric circles over the surface. Sprinkle the olives over them, followed by pepper and the optional red pepper flakes.

Bake for 10 minutes, or until the bottom of the crust is golden. Remove from the oven, then scatter the basil over the surface. Let stand for a minute or two, then cut into 6 wedges and serve.

16. VEGAN MEXICAN PIZZA

Layer on the Southwestern flavors in this playful vegan Mexican pizza. It starts with refried beans (in place of red sauce), followed by salsa, corn and nondairy cheese. Serve with a colorful green salad and garlic-sautéed greens. This recipe doubles easily. Adapted from Vegan Express.

Makes: 6 slices

One 12- to 14-inch good-quality pizza crust, or Basic Pizza Dough

1 cup (about half of a 16-ounce can) vegan refried beans,

(I like Annie's organic refried beans with green chili in the

BPA-free can) or homemade Refried Beans

1 cup mild or medium-hot salsa, your favorite variety

1 cup grated cheddar or Jack-style nondairy cheese

1/2 to 3/4 cup frozen organic corn kernels, thawed

1 to 2 scallions, sliced

1 fresh hot chili pepper, seeded and sliced, optional

Place the crust on a pan. Spread it with the refried beans (thin canned refried beans with a tiny bit of water if need be, to make them more spreadable, depending on the brand), then the salsa.

Sprinkle with the cheese and corn kernels, followed by the scallions and optional chili pepper.

Bake until the cheese is bubbly, about 8 to 10 minutes. Remove from the oven, let stand for 2 to 3 minutes, and cut into 6 wedges to serve.

17. VERDANT VEGGIE PESTO PIZZA

If you like a very veggie-filled pizza, this one's for you, piled generously with broccoli, bell pepper, and zucchini. And in place of the usual tomato sauce, this one features a delectable spinach-miso pesto as the base.

Makes: 6 slices

Spinach-miso pesto:

4 to 5 ounces fresh baby spinach

1/4 cup fresh basil leaves

1/4 cup fresh parsley leaves

1/4 cup untoasted walnuts or raw cashews

2 scallions, green parts only

1 to 2 tablespoons miso, preferably mellow white, to taste

1 1/2 cups small broccoli florets

1 medium green bell pepper, cut into narrow, short strips

3/4 cup thinly sliced rounds from a small zucchini

1 to 2 medium tomatoes,

3 to 4 cloves garlic, sliced

1 tablespoon extra-virgin olive oil

One 12- to 14-inch good-quality pizza crust

1 1/2 cups mozzarella-style nondairy cheese

Preheat the oven to 425 degrees F.

Combine the ingredients for the pesto in a food processor. Process until smoothly pureed, stopping the machine and scraping down the sides as needed.

Combine the broccoli florets, bell pepper, zucchini, and garlic in a mixing bowl and drizzle in the olive oil. Stir together. Transfer the vegetables to a lightly oiled roasting pan and put in the oven. Stir after 10 minutes, and continue to roast until the vegetables are touched with brown spots here and there.

Meanwhile spread the pesto on the pizza crust, then sprinkle evenly with the cheese. Bake for 15 minutes, or until the cheese is nicely melted. Remove from the oven, let stand for a minute, then cut into 6 wedges (it's easier to cut the pizza before piling on the veggies).

When the vegetables are done, distribute them evenly over the surface of the pizza. If the pizza came out of the oven an few minutes before the vegetables, put the whole thing back into the oven for a couple of minutes, just so that everything can be piping hot, then serve at once.

18. ARUGULA SALAD PIZZA

Here's how you rethink your plate: a fresh green salad and whole grain pizza all in one meal that you can whip up in 45 minutes. Arugula salad pizza is a quick and delicious vegan treat for even the busiest night of your week! It's great served with a simple soup.

Serves: 8 (1 slice each)

Whole grain pizza dough (see Notes), or one 16-ounce package refrigerated whole grain pizza dough, or whole grain pizza dough prepared from a mix

Cornmeal for sprinkling

1/3 cup marinara sauce

1½ teaspoons dried oregano

1 cup shredded plant-based cheese (see Notes)

2 cups mixed fresh arugula and baby spinach

1½ cups fresh yellow cherry tomatoes halved

½ medium red bell pepper, diced

1 ripe medium avocado, sliced

¼ cup roasted pistachios

1 tablespoon balsamic vinegar

1 tablespoon extra virgin olive oil

Preheat the oven to 350°F.

Roll out the pizza dough to fit a 14-inch pizza pan or pizza stone. Sprinkle the pan or stone with cornmeal and fit the dough on top.

Spread the marinara sauce onto the dough and sprinkle the oregano and plant-based cheese over it. Place the pan or stone in the oven and bake for 30 to 35 minutes, until the crust is golden and firm to the touch.

At the last minute before serving, remove the crust from the oven and top with the arugula and spinach, tomatoes, bell pepper, avocado, and pistachios. The greens will wilt quickly.

Drizzle with the vinegar and olive oil. Serve immediately.

Notes:

You may prepare your own pizza dough following this procedure: Stir together ¾ cup warm (110°F) water, 1½ teaspoons active dry yeast, and 1 teaspoon honey in a medium bowl. Let stand for 10 minutes.

Stir in 1½ teaspoons extra virgin olive oil and 1¾ cups whole wheat flour. Tip the dough onto a lightly floured surface and knead for 10 minutes.

Place the dough in an oiled bowl, cover with a towel, and let it rise in a warm place for about 1 hour, then proceed with step 1 of the recipe. Omit the plant-based cheese, if desired.

Variation: Substitute other firm greens, such as baby kale or chopped collard greens, for the arugula and baby spinach.

19. MIXED OLIVES AND SPINACH PIZZA

Olives add great flavor to this vegan spinach pizza. It features a generous helping of baby spinach; or, you can use baby arugula instead. Do try this with pepper jack or other spicy vegan cheese, which gives it a bit of a kick. Serve with a colorful salad — add some beans or chickpeas for more protein.

Makes: 6 wedges, 2 wedges per serving

One 12- to 14-inch good-quality pizza crust
1 cup good-quality marinara or pizza sauce, more or less as needed

1 to 1 1/2 cups grated mozzarella-style or pepperjack vegan cheese

2 to 3 big handfuls of baby spinach or arugula

enough to cover the surface generously

1/3 cup chopped green olives

1/3 cup chopped black olives

Dried hot red pepper flakes to taste, optional

Preheat the oven to 425° F.

Place the crust on a pan, spread the sauce evenly over it, and sprinkle with the cheese.

Bake until the cheese is bubbly and the bottom of the crust is golden, about 8 to 10 minutes.

Sprinkle with the spinach or arugula, followed by the olives, and return to the oven just until the greens wilt down, which should take less than a minute. Remove from the oven, and sprinkle with dried hot red pepper flakes, or pass them around, if you haven't used spicy cheese.

Let the pizza stand for a minute or two, and cut into 6 wedges to serve.

Tip: If you don't have a pizza stone and pizza wheel, try cutting the crust with kitchen sheers even before putting the toppings on. Makes it so much easier to deal with when it comes out of the hot oven!

Variation: Make this a white pizza by replacing the red sauce with pureed silken tofu.

20. WHITE PIZZA WITH SWEET POTATO, ONIONS, AND OLIVES

Here's a delectably different kind of pizza—a vegan white pizza brimming with well-cooked onions, roasted sweet potato, and briny olives. Combined with most any kind of salad, this pizza makes a delicious cool-weather dinner. This makes 6 to 8 slices. Double the recipe if you're feeding more than 3 hungry people! Photos by Evan Atlas.

Ingredients

1½ tablespoons olive oil

2 large onions, quartered and thinly sliced (use yellow or red, or one of each)

3 to 4 cloves garlic, thinly sliced

1 large sweet potato (see Note)

2 teaspoons olive oil

Half of one 12.3-ounce package firm silken tofu

2 tablespoons unsweetened nondairy milk

½ teaspoon salt

Good-quality 12- to 14-ounce pizza crust

1 cup vegan mozzarella-style shredded cheese, such as Daiya

⅓ cup oil-cured pitted black olives, such as Kalamata, chopped

Leaves from a sprig of fresh rosemary, or dried rosemary to taste

Instructions

Heat the oil in a medium skillet. Add the onions and sauté over medium-low heat until limp. Add the garlic and continue to sauté until the onion is deep golden, stirring frequently, about 15 minutes.

Preheat the oven to 425 degrees F.

While the onions are cooking, peel the sweet potato and cut into small dice. Place in a small mixing bowl and toss with the olive oil.

Arrange the sweet potato dice in a lightly oiled or parchment-lined small baking pan. Bake for 15 minutes, or until just tender and lightly roasted, about 15 minutes. Stir every 5 minutes or so. Remove from the oven when done.

Puree the tofu with the nondairy milk and salt in a food processor or with a an immersion blender in its container.

Place the crust on a baking sheet or a pizza stone. Spread the pureed tofu evenly over the surface of the crust with a baking spatula. Sprinkle with the vegan cheese.

Layer the onion mixture evenly over the cheese layer. Scatter the roasted sweet potato pieces over the onion layer, followed by the olives.

Bake for 12 to 15 minutes, or until the crust is golden. Cut into 6 to 8 slices and serve.

Note: If you have a baked sweet potato on hand, or if you just want to pre-bake it in the microwave oven until done but still a little firm, that's fine, too, and you can skip the step of roasting it.

21. VEGAN ONION AND OLIVE PIZZA

This deliciously offbeat onion and olive pizza features mellow caramelized onions, with briny olives for a contrasting flavor. For a simple meal, serve with a salad of mixed greens, cannellini or chickpeas, and ripe tomatoes.

Makes 6 slices

1 1/2 tablespoons extra-virgin olive oil

1 large red onion, quartered and thinly sliced

1 large white or yellow onion, quartered and thinly sliced

2 cloves garlic, minced

4 to 6 ounces grated nondairy cheese, variety of your choice

12-inch good-quality prepared pizza crust

1/2 cup chopped black olives, preferably cured (such as Kalamata)

Dried thyme or oregano

Heat the oil in a large skillet. Add the onions and sauté slowly, covered, until translucent. Uncover, add the garlic and continue to sauté until they are nicely golden (but not browned), stirring often.

Sprinkle the cheese evenly the pizza crust, followed by over the onions and olives. Finish with a sprinkling of thyme or oregano.

Bake in a preheated 425 degree F. oven for 10 minutes, or until the cheese is melted and the bottom of the crust is golden.

Remove from the oven, and allow to sit for 2 to 3 minutes. Cut into wedges and serve.

22. VEGAN ROASTED VEGGIE PIZZA

This hearty vegan roasted veggie pizza is a good one for hearty appetites. Feeding a larger crowd? The recipe is easily doubled to make two pizzas. Vary the pizza with other vegetables you may have on hand, including eggplant, sweet potato, kale, yellow summer squash, etc.

Makes: 6 slices

1 link Tofurky or Field Roast vegan sausage, sliced 1/4 inch thick

1 medium red bell pepper, cut into narrow strips

1 1/2 cups small broccoli florets

1 small zucchini, sliced (or about 1 cup halved and sliced zucchini)

2 tablespoons sliced sun dried tomatoes, optional

1 tablespoon olive oil

3/4 cup good-quality pizza or marinara sauce,

your favorite all-natural brand or homemade Classic Marinara Sauce, or as needed

One good-quality 12- to 14-ounce pizza crust, or Basic Pizza Dough (see note)

3/4 to 1 cup grated nondairy cheddar- or mozzarella-style cheese, optional

Dried basil

Preheat the oven to 425 degrees F.

Combine the sausage, bell pepper, broccoli, zucchini, optional dried tomatoes, and oil in a mixing bowl. Stir together and transfer to a lightly oiled roasting pan. Place in the hot oven.

Meanwhile, place the crust on a pizza stone or on a baking sheet. Distribute the sauce over the surface of the crust. Sprinkle with the optional cheese. Cut the pizza into 6 slices (use a pizza wheel if on a stone; kitchen shears if on a baking sheet). Place the pizza in the oven about 10 minutes after the vegetables.

Give the vegetables a stir after the pizza crust goes in the oven. Bake for a additional 12 to 15 minutes, or until the vegetables are nicely roasted and the pizza crust begins to turn golden.

Distribute the vegetable mixture evenly over the surface of the pizza, then serve at once.

Note: The Basic Pizza Dough recipe on this site makes enough for two crusts, so you can either halve the recipe, or go ahead and make the entire batch and make two pizzas while you're at it! Pizza generally freezes well.

23. VEGAN WHITE PIZZA WITH ASPARAGUS AND SPINACH

Here's a light, lively vegan white pizza recipe that's perfect for a springtime meal. It features favorite spring veggies — asparagus and spinach on a creamy backdrop. Serve with a big green salad; toss in some chickpeas, whose flavor is highly compatible with the pizza. This pizza goes down easy, so double the recipe if you're serving a hungry group.

Ingredients

12 asparagus spears

4 to 5 ounces fresh baby spinach

12.3-ounce package firm silken tofu

1 teaspoon salt

One good-quality 12- to 14-ounce pizza crust

⅓ cup sun-dried tomatoes cut into strips

1 cup mozzarella-style nondairy cheese, optional

Instructions

Preheat the oven to 425 degrees F.

Trim about an inch from the bottom of the asparagus spears. Scrape the bottom halves if you'd like, though if they're very slender, this won't be necessary. Cut the spears into 1-inch pieces. Steam the asparagus with a little water in a covered skillet until bright green and just barely tender-crisp.

Add the spinach and cover; steam until just wilted, about a minute. Drain the asparagus and spinach well.

Puree the tofu with the salt in a food processor or with an immersion blender in its container.

Place the crust on a baking sheet or a pizza stone. Spread the tofu puree evenly over the surface of the crust with a baking spatula.

Scatter the asparagus and spinach evenly over the surface of the pizza, followed by the dried tomatoes. Bake for 12 to 15 minutes, or until the crust is golden. Cut into 6 slices or 8 slices and serve.

24. SHEPHERD'S PIE PIZZA

Some people are born to rock 'n' roll. Others are born to ride. I was born to put mashed potatoes on pizza. I've done it so many ways I can't even remember them all, but this was my favorite. Mashed potatoes, carrots, peas, and plenty of savory herbs make an unusually hearty cross between shepherd's pie and pizza.

Makes: One 14-inch pizza

1 prepared whole-grain 14-inch pizza crust

"Sauce":

1 pound Yukon Gold potatoes

½ cup finely chopped red onion

2 cloves garlic, minced

Splash of oil, for sautéing

¼ cup plain vegan creamer (soy or coconut) or nondairy milk

2 tablespoons vegan margarine

½ teaspoon dried rosemary

½ teaspoon dried thyme

Topping:

1 carrot, diced

½ cup peas (fresh or frozen)

½ cup chopped cauliflower

½ cup green beans

½ cup sliced mushrooms

2 tablespoons vegan margarine

2 tablespoons all-purpose flour

½ cup vegetable broth

2 tablespoons chopped fresh sage

Salt and freshly ground black pepper

Preheat your oven to 450° F, bake the pizza crust for 3 to 4 minutes, then remove from the oven, leaving the stone inside, and set aside.

Make the "sauce": Peel the potatoes and cut into ½-inch dice. Place in a saucepan and cover with cold water. Cover the pan and over high heat, bring the water to a boil. Then lower the temperature to a simmer and cook the potatoes until you can easily smash them with a fork or tongs, 15 to 20 minutes.

Sauté the onion and garlic with a splash of oil in a small pan over medium heat, until tender, 3 to 5 minutes.

Drain the potatoes and place them in a large bowl with the garlic, onion, soy creamer, margarine, rosemary, and thyme. Use a potato masher to mash everything together—some lumps are fine! (You can also use a food processor, but be aware that will result in a gluey mashed potato!)

Make the topping: Steam the carrot, peas, cauliflower and green beans until tender. In a large saucepan over medium heat, combine the steamed veggies, mushrooms, margarine, flour, vegetable broth, sage, and salt and pepper to taste. Cook until thick sauce forms, about 3 minutes, and set aside.

Spread the potato mixture over the pizza crust and top with the vegetables and salt and pepper to taste.

Bake for 15 to 20 minutes, until everything is warm and toasty. Let stands for a couple of minutes, then cut into 8 wedges to serve.

This hearty vegan roasted veggie pizza is a good one for hearty appetites. Feeding a larger crowd? The recipe is easily doubled to make two pizzas. Vary the pizza with other vegetables you may have on hand, including eggplant, sweet potato, kale, yellow summer squash, etc.

Makes: 6 slices

1 link Tofurky or Field Roast vegan sausage, sliced 1/4 inch thick

1 medium red bell pepper, cut into narrow strips

1 1/2 cups small broccoli florets

1 small zucchini, sliced (or about 1 cup halved and sliced zucchini)

2 tablespoons sliced sun dried tomatoes, optional

1 tablespoon olive oil

3/4 cup good-quality pizza or marinara sauce, your favorite all-natural brand or homemade Classic Marinara Sauce, or as needed

One good-quality 12- to 14-ounce pizza crust, or Basic Pizza Dough (see note)

3/4 to 1 cup grated nondairy cheddar- or mozzarella-style cheese, optional

Dried basil

Preheat the oven to 425 degrees F.

Combine the sausage, bell pepper, broccoli, zucchini, optional dried tomatoes, and oil in a mixing bowl. Stir together and transfer to a lightly oiled roasting pan. Place in the hot oven.

Meanwhile, place the crust on a pizza stone or on a baking sheet. Distribute the sauce over the surface of the crust. Sprinkle with the optional cheese. Cut the pizza into 6 slices (use a pizza wheel if on a stone; kitchen shears if on a baking sheet). Place the pizza in the oven about 10 minutes after the vegetables.

Give the vegetables a stir after the pizza crust goes in the oven. Bake for an additional 12 to 15 minutes, or until the vegetables are nicely roasted and the pizza crust begins to turn golden.

Distribute the vegetable mixture evenly over the surface of the pizza, then serve at once.

Note: The Basic Pizza Dough recipe on this site makes enough for two crusts, so you can either halve the recipe, or go ahead and make the entire batch and make two pizzas while you're at it! Pizza generally freezes well.

25. POLENTA PIZZA CRUST VEGAN

While I love homemade pizza, I look for shortcuts to replace a dough-based crust. Though it's gluten-free, you need not follow a GF diet to enjoy this change-of-pace polenta pizza crust.

Ingredients

1 tube (18-ounce) prepared organic polenta, broken in pieces

1 cup cooked and cooled brown rice

½ cup chickpea flour (or use ½ cup plus 2 tablespoons millet flour)

½ teaspoon garlic powder

¼ scant teaspoon salt

1 tablespoon cornmeal

Instructions

Preheat oven to 425°F. If you have a pizza stone, place it in the oven.

If you don't, have a pizza pan or other large baking pan at hand (but it doesn't need to preheat).

In a food processor, add the polenta, rice, chickpea flour, garlic powder, and sea salt and pulse first to combine, then process just until the mixture comes together in a ball on the blade.

Remove the dough ball and place it on a large sheet of parchment paper. Cover with another piece of parchment. Roll out the dough with a rolling pin between the parchment sheets to about 12" diameter or more, and ½" thick.

Remove the top sheet of parchment from the dough. Using a pizza peel or a very large tray/plate, transfer the pizza crust to the pizza stone (with the single layer of parchment still underneath the dough).

Bake for 25 minutes until it is golden around the edges and firm in the center. Remove the pizza stone to let the crust cool slightly for few minutes while preparing the toppings.

When ready to bake, increase oven temperature to 450°F. Using a large plate or your pizza peel, remove the crust from the pizza stone/ pan and invert to remove the parchment.

Sprinkle the cornmeal over stone/pan, and place on pizza. Add toppings (see suggestions), and bake for 13 to 15 minutes, until heated through, and longer if desired for crispier edges/crust. Remove, let sit for 3 to 5 minutes, then serve.

27. PUFFED BUCKWHEAT GRANOLA FRUIT PIZZA VEGAN

This granola pizza is a perfect weekend brunch number & a great healthy snack if you've got the munchies (I have them all the time if you know me well). I also tried freezing it, which worked, although the base became a bit soft and more crumbly. I used puffed buckwheat in this recipe (it's been sat in my cupboard for weeks now and I hardly used it as it's so bland on its own) and carob powder instead of cacao to make it lower fat and also caffeine-free. Have a great hump day everyone and stay healthy and active

RECIPE

Granola pizza recipe:

Ingredients:

1/2 cup (gluten free) oats

1 cup puffed buckwheat

1/4 cup almond flakes

1/4 cup unsweetened desiccated coconut

1/4 cup coconut oil, melted

1/4 cup + 2 tbsp water

3 tbsp carob powder

Optional: 1-2 tsbp sweetener of choice (like maple or date syrup) if you prefer a sweeter taste.

Directions:

1. Preheat the oven to 180C (350F) & line a baking tray with parchment paper. You might want to brush the parchment paper with a little coconut oil to prevent the pizza sticking to the sheet.

2. Place all the ingredients in a food processor and blend until the mixture resembles slightly sticky 'dough' consistency (around 3-5 minutes). 3. Scoop out the texture onto the baking tray lined with parchment paper and gently press with your hands to flatten it out into a circle (around 3 inches thick). 4. Bake in the oven at 180C (350F) for 13-15 minutes until the pizza is slightly brown on the edges.

3. Top with coconut yogurt (or nut butter) and your choice of fruit toppings.

28. GRILLED EGGPLANT PIZZA BURGER

The Pizza Burger. Flat Grilled Buns layered between grilled eggplant, red bell pepper, grilled mock chick'n, olives, spinach, sundried tomato sauce & melty vegan cheese. Holla.

RECIPE

Vegan Pizza Burger

Ingredients:

1 tbsp oil of choice for grilling

3-4 slices of seitan

2 thin slices of eggplant

2 thin slices of red bell pepper

3 pitted black Spanish olives, sliced

Spinach leaves

3x slightly flat hamburger buns

1 tbsp vegan butter

Sundried Tomato Sauce

1/3 cup sundried tomatoes (drained from any oil)

1/3 cup tomato paste

1 tbsp coconut sugar

1 tsp onion powder

1 tsp garlic powder

salt to taste

water as needed

Vegan Melted Cheese

1 tbsp vegan butter

1 tbsp flour

2 tbsp Nutritional Yeast

1/2 cup + 2 tbsp rice or soy milk (plus more if needed)

1 tsp lemon juice

1 tsp onion powder

1/2 tsp garlic powder

salt & pepper to taste

Directions:

Prep the Sundried Tomato Sauce first by blending everything in a food processor or blender. Add a little water as necessary to get the blades moving. Set aside.

Grill the seitan in a small frying pan with a little oil until all sides are crispy. Lay the slices on a paper towel to drain from any excess oil & liquid.

Heat up some oil on a grill plate or a large frying pan and grill the red bell pepper and eggplant until charred. (I would recommend doing the bell pepper first, as it takes a little longer to cook than the eggplant)

Follow the same procedure as the seitan and transfer to a paper towel to drain the oil/liquid.

To prep your 'melted cheese' simply melt the vegan butter in a small sauce pan. Add the flour and whisk until it forms a roux. Slowly begin adding the milk, stirring continuously after each addition until it begins to resemble melted cheese. Reduce the heat and whisk in the nutritional yeast, lemon juice and spices until well combined. Adjust the consistency by adding more milk if needed. Remove from the heat.

Grill the buns on both sides some vegan butter. (I flattened mine out a little using a spatula to resemble 'pizza bases'.

To assemble, neatly layer and assert some spinach, eggplant, capsicum, seitan slices, olives and a little drizzle of the melty cheese on the base. I double layered mine so used half the ingredients on one layer, and the rest on the top layer (However, you could just do one layer!)

Enjoy!

29. MAC N' CHEESE PIZZA VEGAN

Mac n' Cheese Pizza...want a slice? Or want to make your own?!? Well, you can, because I've teamed up my amazing friend, plant based health. This totally decadent mac n' cheese pizza is made of entirely healthy plant based ingredients, including Banza chickpea elbows which are soy free, vegan, non-gmo, and certified gluten free!

Mac n' Cheese Pizza

Cook 1 package of Banza elbows according to package directions. While pasta cooks, prepare cheeze sauce.

For the Cheeze Sauce:

1 cup cooked Japanese sweet potato (with the yellow inside)

1/2 cup unsweetened non-dairy milk

1/2 cup nutritional yeast

1 tsp garlic powder

2/3 tsp smoked paprika

1/2 tsp black salt (or sea salt)

Blend in a high speed blender or food processor until creamy. Add additional plant based milk by the tablespoon until desired consistency is reached. Mix cooked pasta in cheeze sauce. Set aside.

Prepare your favorite gluten free pizza crust and sauce.

Put a layer of pizza sauce on your crust and then add a nice layer of the mac n' cheese. Bake at 400 degrees for 10 minutes or until edges are brown. Serve any leftover mac n' cheese on the side with a huge raw salad!

30. MINI VEGAN TORTILLA PIZZAS

I think this would also work as dessert pizzas, by just swapping out sauce, cheese and pizza toppings, and instead baking she shells, then putting melted chocolate and fresh fruit inside, freezing until semi-firm, and topping with coconut whipped cream.

You can put on any kind of toppings you want – that's what makes pizza so freakin' amazing. It's versatile.

INGREDIENTS

8 small flour tortillas (corn may work too, but I haven't tried)

1 cup tomato sauce

cheese of choice (I used, vegan parmesan, Daiya shreds, and nacho cheese sauce)

toppings of choice (I used green lentils, green pepper, kalamata olives, and zucchini)

INSTRUCTIONS

Preheat oven to 375F. Spray 2 muffins tins with non-stick cooking spray (or use refined coconut oil) and set aside.

31. VEGAN BROCCOLI RABE & CASHEW RICOTTA WHITE PIZZA

A note on the crust is in order. I generally consider myself pretty ambitious in my kitchenery, but there are some things that just take more time than I'm generally willing to give. Pizza crust would be one of those things. I'll make a yeast bread from time to time if the yeast bread is the end product I'm going for. In this case, I was going for dinner, so quick and easy were top priorities. I was fortunate enough to get my hands on some vegan bread dough, which worked like a charm. You might be so lucky as to find vegan pizza dough, which would be even better, or a pre-made vegan pizza shell. If you're up for making your own dough, here's a recipe to try. Another thing I've done is use naan as a pizza crust. This will give you a bunch of one or two serving size pizzas, so make sure you buy about four loaves

Ingredients

For the Crust

1 vegan pizza crust of choice (store bought or homemade)

1 Tbsp. olive oil (unless your crust is pre-baked)

For the Cashew Ricotta

1/2 cup raw cashews, soaked in water 4-8 hours and drained

3 tbsp. lemon juice

2 Tbsp. unflavored soy or almond milk

1/4 lb. extra firm tofu, drained

For the Broccoli Rabe

2 tbsp. olive oil

4 garlic cloves, minced

1 1/2 lb. broccoli rabe, stems removed and chopped into 1-2 inch pieces

1/2 tsp. salt

1/2 Tsp. pepper

1/2 Tsp. red pepper flakes (or to taste)

Instructions

Prepare the Crust

If starting with dough crust, brush with 1 tablespoon of olive oil and bake per recipe instructions. If using a pre-baked shell, use as-is or heat in a 400° oven for an few minutes.

Make the Cashew Ricotta

Place cashews in blender or food processor and blend to a smooth paste.

Add lemon juice and milk. Blend until smooth.

Add tofu and pulse an few times to blend. Keep the texture chunky.

Prepare the Broccoli Rabe

Fill a large pot with water and bring to a boil. Add broccoli rabe and boil just until it begins to tenderize and turns bright green, about 1-2 minutes.

Drain and immediately rinse with cold water. Press out any excess water.

Heat oil in a large skillet or pot (you can use the same pot) over medium heat. Add garlic and saute for 1 minute.

Add broccoli rabe. Sautee until tender, about 3 minutes. Add salt, pepper and red pepper flakes.

Assemble the Pizza

Arrange broccoli rabe in an even layer over crust. Top with cashew ricotta in 1-2 tablespoon dollops.

Using a doughnut cutter or small drinking glass, cut out your mini pizzas from the tortillas. I placed mine over the muffin tin first, to see how big to make my pizzas. You wants them to be a bit bigger than the opening of the hole.

Place your tortilla pizzas inside your muffin tins, pressing down gently.

Add a bit of sauce, then cheese, then toppings, to each tortilla pizza.

Bake for about 15 minutes, or until the tortilla is a nice golden brown color, and the sauce & toppings are warm and the cheese has melted.

Allow to cool for about 5 minutes. If you handle them too early, they may not pop out of the tins easily.

Run a butter knife around each pizza, and pop it out - but only if it's ready. If it doesn't come out easily, let it cool for an few more minutes.

32.VEGAN MOZZARELLA MAC DEEP DISH PIZZA

Creamy mozzarella mac 'n' cheese in a delicious, homemade deep dish crust with easy toppings and flavorful marinara.

Ingredients

Pizza Crust

½ C. Warm Water

1 tsp. Sugar

1 T . Active Dry Yeast

1 C . Unbleached All-Purpose Flour You may need to add more in while kneading

½ C. Whole Wheat Flour

1 tsp. Dried Italian Seasoning

½ Tsp. Garlic Powder

1/2 Tsp. Italian Seasoning

Corn Meal for Dusting

2 T . Olive Oil + Extra for Brushing

Mozzarella Mac

2 C . Dried Pasta, I used Shells and they worked perfectly!

1 1/2 C. Daiya Mozzarella Shreds

1/2 C. Raw Cashews Soaked for at least 30 minutes

1/2 C. Vegetable Broth or Water

Marinara

1 1/2 C . Tomato Sauce

1 T . Tomato Paste

1/2 tsp . Dried Italian Seasoning

1/2 tsp . Garlic Powder

Salt to taste

Toppings (Optional and Interchangeable)

1-2 C. Baby Kale or Whatever Greens you prefer

1/2 C. Quartered Artichoke Hearts

1/4 C. Pitted and Sliced Black Olives

3 T . Sun-dried Tomatoes Julienne-Cut

Instructions

Pizza Crust & Assembly

Stir the sugar and active dry yeast into the warm water until it dissolves. Set aside and let it rise for 12-25 minutes.

Sift the dry ingredients together in a large bowl. Once the yeast is ready, pour it into the bowl, along with the olive oil. Knead the dough on a surface dusted with flour, for 3 minutes.

Place the dough ball in an oiled bowl, cover with a damp cloth, for 30 minutes.

(Start on the mac 'n' cheese and marinara)

Preheat oven for 425°F.

Take the raised dough and knead for another 1-2 minutes. Roll out flat, to about 1/4" thick; then carefully stretch the dough out with your hands until it is about 14"wide.

Press the dough into a 9" springform pan that has a light coating of oil, and bake for 5 minutes. Keep an eye on the crust to make sure that no large air bubbles form. If they do, carefully poke them with a knife.

Take the crust out of the oven, spread the mozzarella mac out over the bottom, layer the toppings and end with the marinara sauce and brush a little olive oil onto the crust. Bake for an additional 18-20 minutes.

Once the crust is nice and golden, let the pizza cool for a couple of minutes and take off the springform wall.

Slice with a sharp knife and serve!

Mozzarella Mac

Cook the pasta according to the package instructions, drain and then rinse in cool water.

Puree the Daiya shreds, cashews, and vegetable broth in a blender until completely smooth. Seriously, suuuper smooth.

Place the pasta back in a pot over low-medium heat and stir in the mozzarella mixture. Cook for 5 minutes, then set aside until the crust is baked.

Marinara

Place all of the ingredients into a small pan over medium heat. Stir until evenly combined and simmer for 3-5 minutes to thicken slightly.

Take off of heat and set aside until ready to use.

33. WHOLE WHEAT ROASTED VEGGIE & TEMPEH PIZZA.

Recipe for a vegan Whole Wheat Roasted Veggie & Tempeh Pizza. Very rustic and super delicious. You won't even miss cheese on this pizza!

Ingredients for the pizza dough

2 1/2 cups whole-wheat flour

1/2 teaspoon salt

1/2 teaspoon active dry yeast

2/3 cup warm water

1 tablespoon olive oil

1 pinch sugar

Ingredients for the toppings

3/4 cup tomato purée*

1/4 teaspoon liquid smoke

1/4 teaspoon salt + more for the veggies & tempeh

1/8 teaspoon garlic powder

1/4 teaspoon sriracha Sauce

1/2 eggplant

1/2 zucchini

5 slices tempeh

4 cups mushrooms

olive oil for the pan

1/4 teaspoon paprika powder

Few twigs fresh oregano

Instructions

For the pizza dough, put all the ingredients in a bread baking machine (use the dough program), kitchen machine or mix by hand and let it rise until it doubles in size.

Preheat the oven on full heat.

Form two balls with the dough and roll each of it out until it's a nice pizza base. At this step, I already put the pizza base on a baking sheet and try to make things easier afterward.

Mix the tomato purée with the Liquid Smoke, salt, garlic powder & Sriracha Sauce and spread it over the pizza base.

Cut the eggplant and zucchini in thin slices and roast them in a pan with a bit of oil and salt for a few minutes and set aside.

Cut the tempeh in slices and in half. Pan-fry them with a bit of salt & paprika powder for an few minutes and set aside.

Wash & cut the mushrooms in thin slices and roast them in the pan until they lose most of their water.

Place the mushrooms, eggplant, zucchini and tempeh on the pizza and put it in the oven for about 20 minutes.

Top with fresh oregano once it's ready & enjoy!

CHAPTER 2

GLUTEN FREE PIZZA

1. GLUTEN-FREE PIZZA

Challenged with a gluten-free diet and a pizza craving? Make our cheesy pizza thanks to Bisquick Gluten Free mix.

Ingredients

1 1/3 cups Bisquick Gluten Free mix

1/2 teaspoon Italian seasoning or dried basil

1/2 cup water

1/3 cup oil

2 eggs, beaten

Suggested Topping Quantities:

1 can (8 oz) pizza sauce

1 cup bite-size pieces favorite meat or vegetables

1 1/2 cups shredded mozzarella cheese (6 oz)

Steps

Heat oven to 425°F. Grease 12-inch pizza pan. Stir Bisquick mix, Italian seasoning, water, oil and eggs until well combined; spread in pan.

Bake 15 minutes (crust will appear cracked).

Spread pizza sauce over crust; top with meat and cheese.

Bake 10 to15 minutes longer or until cheese is melted.

2. GLUTEN-FREE MARGHERITA PIZZA

Less is more when it comes to this pizza-- simple sauce with minimal toppings.

Ingredients

Crust

1 package fast-acting dry yeast

2/3 cup water (105° to 115°F)

1 tablespoon extra-virgin olive oil

1 egg white

1 1/4 cups Betty Crocker All-Purpose Gluten Free Rice Flour Blend

1 tablespoon sugar

1 teaspoon xanthan gum

1/2 teaspoon salt

Topping

1/2 cup canned crushed tomatoes, undrained (from 14- to 15-oz can)

1 teaspoon extra-virgin olive oil

1teaspoon finely chopped garlic

1/4 teaspoon salt

1/8teaspoon pepper

1/4cup fresh basil leaves, cut into thin strips

1/4 cup finely shredded gluten-free Parmesan cheese

4 oz fresh mozzarella cheese, cut into 1/4-inch slices

Steps

1. In large bowl, stir together yeast and water; let stand 5 minutes. Stir in 1 tablespoon oil and the egg white. Stir in 1 1/4 cups flour blend, the sugar, xanthan gum and 1/2 teaspoon salt. Cover with plastic wrap. Let stand in warm place 1 hour.

2. Generously grease 12-inch pizza pan or large cookie sheet. Place dough on a pan. Press into 11-inch circle. Cover; let rise 30 minutes. Heat oven to 425°

3. With wet fingers, press dough into 12-inch circle. Bake 10 to 12 minutes or until edges begin to brown. Increase oven temperature to 450°F.

4. In a small bowl, stir together tomatoes, 1 teaspoon oil, the garlic, 1/4 teaspoon salt and the pepper. Spread evenly over pre-baked crust to within 1/2 inch of edge. Sprinkle with basil and Parmesan cheese. Divide mozzarella evenly over crust. Bake about 8 minutes longer or until cheese is bubbly and edge is golden brown. Let stands 1 to 2 minutes before slicing.

3. GLUTEN-FREE BROWNIE AND BERRIES DESSERT PIZZA

Want to wow a chocolate-craving crowd? Make a sweet dessert pizza topped with a creamy layer and tart berries.

Ingredients

1 box Betty Crocker Gluten Free brownie mix

Butter and eggs called for on brownie mix box

1 package (8 oz) cream cheese, softened

1/3 cup sugar

1/2 teaspoon vanilla

2 cups sliced fresh strawberries

1 cup fresh blueberries

1 cup fresh raspberries

1/2 cup apple jelly

Steps

1. Heat oven to 350°F (or 325°F for dark or nonstick pan). Grease bottom only of 12-inch pizza pan with cooking spray or shortening.
2. In large bowl, stir brownie mix, butter and eggs until well blended. Spread in a pan.
3. Bake 18 to 20 minutes or until toothpick inserted 2 inches from side of pan comes out clean or almost clean. Cool completely, about 1 hour.
4. In a small bowl, beat cream cheese, sugar, and vanilla with electric mixer on medium speed until smooth. Spread mixture evenly over brownie base. Arrange berries over cream cheese mixture. Stir jelly until smooth; brush over berries. Refrigerate about 1 hour or until chilled. Cut into wedges. Store covered in the refrigerator.

4. BANANA SPLIT BROWNIE PIZZA

Get all the goodies of a banana split ice cream dessert with the bonus of fudgy brownies.

Ingredients

1

box (1 lb 6.25 oz) Betty Crocker™ Supreme original brownie mix

Water, vegetable oil and eggs called for on brownie mix box

1 quart (4 cups) favorite flavor ice cream, slightly softened

1 cup sliced fresh strawberries

2 medium bananas, sliced (1 1/2 cups)

1/2 cup chopped fresh pineapple

1/2 cup chopped pecans

1/4 cup Hershey's hot fudge topping

Whipped cream, if desired

Steps

5. Heat oven to 350°F (325°F for dark or nonstick pan). Grease 12x3/4-inch pizza pan with shortening or cooking spray. Make brownie batter as directed on box. Spread in pan.
6. Bake 25 to 28 minutes or until toothpick inserted 2 inches from center comes out almost clean. Cool completely, about 1 hour.
7. Spread slightly softened ice cream evenly over brownies. Freeze at least 1 hour until ice cream is firm. Just before serving, top with strawberries and bananas; sprinkle with pineapple and pecans. Drizzle with topping. Serve with whipped cream.

5. DEEP DISH PIZZA PIE

Original Bisquick mix provides a simple addition to this cheesy pizza baked with pepperoni and veggies – perfect for dinner.

Ingredients

1 lb bulk reduced-fat Italian pork sausage

1 large onion, chopped (1 cup)

1 small green bell pepper, chopped

2 cups Original Bisquick mix

1/2 cup stone-ground yellow cornmeal

1/2 cup shredded Parmesan cheese (2 oz)

6 tablespoons cold butter

1/4 cup boiling water

6 slices (3/4 oz each) mozzarella cheese

2/3 cup pizza sauce

1 package (3 oz) sliced pepperoni

2 cups shredded mozzarella cheese (8 oz)

Small fresh basil leaves, if desired

Steps

1. Heat oven to 350°F. In 12-inch nonstick skillet, cook sausage over medium heat until no longer pink. Remove sausage to paper towels, reserving drippings. Cook onion and bell pepper in drippings until crisp-tender.
2. In a medium bowl, stir Bisquick mix, cornmeal and Parmesan cheese. Cut in butter, using a pastry blender, until crumbly. Add boiling water; stir vigorously until dough forms. Spray 10-inch ovenproof skillet with cooking spray. Press dough on bottom and up side of skillet. Arrange cheese slices over crust; spread with 1/3 cup of the pizza sauce. Top with sausage and onion mixture. Arrange

two-thirds of the pepperoni over onion mixture. Spread remaining 1/3 cup pizza sauce over pepperoni; top with shredded mozzarella cheese and remaining pepperoni.

3. Bake 30 to 35 minutes or until crust is golden brown. Let stands 5 minutes. Garnish with basil. Cut into 8 wedges; serve with additional pizza sauce, heated, if desired.

6. CHICAGO-STYLE DEEP-DISH PIZZA

What is Chicago-style pizza? It's a lofty yeast dough topped lightly with tomato and generous portions of sausage and cheese.

Ingredients

2 packages regular or active dry yeast

1 1/2 cups warm water (105°F to 115°F) SAVE $

6 cups Original Bisquick mix

1/4 cup olive or vegetable oil

8 cups shredded mozzarella cheese (32 oz)

1 lb bulk Italian pork sausage, cooked and drained, or 2 packages (3 1/2 oz each) sliced pepperoni

Vegetable toppings such as sliced fresh mushrooms, chopped green bell pepper or chopped onion, sliced green onions, sliced ripe olives, sliced pimiento-stuffed olives, if desired

2 cans (28 oz each) Muir Glen™ organic whole peeled tomatoes with basil, well drained

2 to 4 tablespoons chopped fresh or 2 teaspoons dried oregano leaves or Italian seasoning

1/2 to 1 cup grated Parmesan cheese

Steps

Move oven racks to lowest positions. Heat oven to 425°F. Grease 2 (15x10x1-inch) pans or 4 (9-inch) round cake pans with olive oil. In a large bowl, dissolve yeast in warm water. Stir in Bisquick mix and oil; beat vigorously 20 strokes. Turn dough onto surface generously dusted with Bisquick mix; gently roll in Bisquick to coat. Knead about 60 times or until smooth and no longer sticky. Let dough rest 5 minutes. (At this point, dough can be covered and refrigerated for up to 24 hours.)

1. Divide dough in half. Pat each half of dough in bottom and up sides of pans. Or divide dough into fourths and press in a bottom and up sides of round pans.

2. Reserve 1 cup of the mozzarella cheese. Sprinkle remaining mozzarella cheese over crusts. Top with sausage, desired vegetable toppings and tomatoes. Sprinkle with oregano and Parmesan cheese. Sprinkle with the reserved mozzarella cheese.

3. 5. Bake 20 to 25 minutes (switching top and bottom pans halfway through bake time) or until crust is brown and cheese is melted and bubbly. Immediately cut pizza into pieces. Let pizzas stand an few minutes for easier serving.

7. GLUTEN-FREE QUICHE LORRAINE PIZZA

You can serve this classic French egg dish, featuring bacon and Swiss, as a main course anytime of the day.

Ingredients

Pastry

1 cup Bisquick Gluten Free mix

1/3 cup plus 1 tablespoon shortening

3 to 4 tablespoons cold water

Filling

8 slices bacon, crisply cooked, crumbled (1/2 cup)

1 cup shredded Swiss cheese (4 oz)

1/3 cup finely chopped onion

4 eggs

2 cups whipping cream or half-and-half

1/4 teaspoon salt

1/4 teaspoon pepper

1/8 teaspoon ground red pepper (cayenne)

Steps

1. Heat oven to 425°F. In medium bowl, cut shortening into Bisquick mix, using pastry blender (or pulling 2 table knives through ingredients in opposite directions) until particles are size of small peas. Sprinkle with cold water, 1 tablespoon at a time, tossing with fork until all flour is moistened and pastry almost cleans side of bowl (1 to 2 teaspoons more water can be added if necessary).

2. Gather pastry into a ball. In a ungreased 9-inch Quiche dish, press pastry evenly in bottom and up sides. Bake 12 to 14 minutes or until pastry just begins to brown and is set.

3. Reduce oven temperature to 325°F. Sprinkle bacon, cheese, and onion into crust. In a medium bowl, beat eggs slightly; beat in remaining filling ingredients. Pour into crust.

4. Bake 45 to 50 minutes or until knife inserted in center comes out clean. Cool 10 minutes before serving.

8. GLUTEN-FREE IMPOSSIBLY EASY BREAKFAST PIZZA

Gluten free cheesy egg pizza? Try our tasty version thanks to Bisquick Gluten Free mix.

Ingredients

1 package (16 oz) bulk pork sausage

1 medium red bell pepper, chopped

1 medium onion, chopped

3 cups frozen hash brown potatoes

2 cups shredded Cheddar cheese (8 oz)

3/4 cup Bisquick Gluten Free mix

2 cups milk

1/4 teaspoon pepper

6 eggs

Steps

1. Heat oven to 400°F. Spray 13x9-inch (3-quart) glass baking dish with cooking spray. In 10-inch skillet, cook sausage, bell pepper and onion over medium heat, stirring occasionally, until sausage is no longer pink; drain. Mix sausage mixture, potatoes and 1 1/2 cups of the cheese in a baking dish.
2. In medium bowl, stir Bisquick mix, milk, pepper, and eggs until blended. Pour over sausage mixture in baking dish.
3. Bake 30 to 35 minutes or until knife inserted in center comes out clean. Sprinkle with remaining 1/2 cup cheese. Bake about 3 minutes longer or until cheese is melted. Let stand 5 minutes before serving.

9. STUFFED-CRUST PEPPERONI PIZZA

Love extra cheese with your pizza? Tuck cheese into the crust for an extra tasty hit.

Ingredients

3 cups Original Bisquick mix

2/3 cup very hot water

2 tablespoons olive or vegetable oil

3/4 cup diced pepperoni

4 sticks Colby-Monterey Jack string cheese (from 10-oz package), cut in half lengthwise

1 can (8 oz) pizza sauce

2 cups shredded Italian cheese blend (8 oz)

1 cup sliced fresh mushrooms

1 small green bell pepper, chopped (1/2 cup)

1 can (2.25 oz) sliced ripe olives, drained

Steps

1. Move oven rack to lowest position; heat oven to 450°F. Spray 12-inch pizza pan with cooking spray. In medium bowl, stir Bisquick mix, hot water, and oil with a fork until soft dough forms; beat vigorously 20 strokes. Let stand 8 minutes.

2. Pat or press dough in bottom and 1 inch over side of pizza pan. Lightly press 1/4 cup of the pepperoni along edge of dough. Place string cheese over pepperoni along edge of dough, overlapping if necessary. Fold 1-inch edge of dough over and around cheese and pepperoni; press to seal. Bake 7 minutes.

3. Spread pizza sauce over partially baked crust. Sprinkle with 1 cup of the Italian cheese, remaining 1/2 cup pepperoni, the mushrooms, bell pepper, and olives. Sprinkle with remaining 1 cup cheese.

4. Bake 9 to 12 minutes longer or until crust is golden brown and cheese is melted.

10. EXTRA-EASY PIZZA

Pizza is always a possibility when you have Bisquick mix on the shelf! Making a crust has never been so quick and easy.

Ingredients

1 1/2 cups Original Bisquick mix

1/3 cup very hot water

1 can (8 ounces) pizza sauce

1 package (3 1/2 ounces) sliced pepperoni

1/2 cup sliced fresh mushroom

1/2 cup chopped bell pepper

1 1/2 cups shredded mozzarella cheese (6 ounces)

Steps

1. Heat oven to 450°F. Grease 12-inch pizza pan. Stir together Bisquick mix and very hot water; beat 20 strokes until soft dough forms.
2. Press dough in pizza pan. Spread pizza sauce over dough. Top with remaining ingredients.
3. Bake 12 to 15 minutes or until crust is golden brown and cheese is bubbly.

Thanks and see you soon!

Copyright © 2017 by Kostya Yaroshenko

All rights reserved.

Printed in Great Britain
by Amazon

43430497R00051